MUSIC FROM THE PAST

£4·50 NID

TUDOR ENGLAND

Arranged for voices and classroom instruments

Alison and Michael Bagenal

D1741118

King Henry VIII at Hampton Court

Hampton Court was one of Henry VIII's many great palaces. The King, his court, his councillors and all his household would visit each palace in turn. There were over 280 rooms always kept ready and richly furnished for guests. The palace stands in a huge park not far from London beside the River Thames. Sometimes the King would arrive by water, having been rowed down the river in the royal barge.

Henry VIII was a man of great physical energy. He was a strong ruler, and also found time for energetic amusements, such as

. . . exercising himself daily in shooting (archery), singing, dancing, wrestling, casting of the bar, playing at the recorders, flute, virginals, and in setting of songs, and making of ballads.

from Edward Halle's The union of the two noble and illustrious famelies of Lancaster and York, 1548

You will notice that music is mentioned. The King loved music and gathered round him a company of singers, instrumentalists, and composers. Here are some of the instruments that he owned:

19 **viols** great and small with three cases of wood covered with black leather.
4 **recorders** of walnut in a case covered with black leather.
a little Venice **lute** with a case.
a **bagge pipe** with pipes of ivory, the bag covered with purple velvet.

from Hayes' King's music, 1937

Look out for pictures of these instruments in this book.

Music for the King's entry

Descant recorder 1
Descant recorder 2 or tenor recorder
Xylophone (D, G, top C)

Drums
Guitar

Entry to the dance, German, 16th century

DESCANT 1

DESCANT 2 OR TENOR RECORDER

G G G G G D D D

G C D G G C D G G

Trumpet and drums would be played when King Henry VIII arrived at Hampton Court Palace and entered the splendid royal rooms.

This music for recorders will sound like trumpets if played grandly, but do not blow too hard or you will play out of tune.

Use at least two large drums to play an introduction and throughout the music. Bounce the drumsticks off the drum for a crisp sound.

Guitar chords are written below the music for the first beat of every bar, the letters also provide a xylophone note for each first beat.

Pastime with good company

Voices
Descant recorder
Tenor recorder
Xylophone (D, E, F♯, G)

Henry VIII

Pas - time with good com - pa - ny I love and shall un - til ___ I die,

Gruch so lust but none ___ de - ny, so God be pleas'd so live ___ will I. For my pas - tance hunt,

sing, and dance my heart ___ is set, To my com - fort all good - ly sport who shall - me let?

As a young man King Henry played the lute, sang, and wrote music. In the evening he danced, sang and made merry with his friends.

This song, and its words, are said to be written by King Henry himself. 'Gruch so lust but none deny' is a good phrase to sing. It means 'Grumble if you will but don't anyone hinder me'. 'Pastance' means 'pastime' and 'Who shall me let?' means 'Who shall stop me?'

You might play the tune on a solo descant recorder first, then use a tenor to play with the voices.

Here is a rhythm for a light drum:

Xylophone accompaniment

4

Green groweth the holly
a trio for two treble recorders and a tenor recorder

from a song by Henry VIII

Wake, wake O man
a duet for tenors or descants

from a hymn by J. Walther, 1490–1570

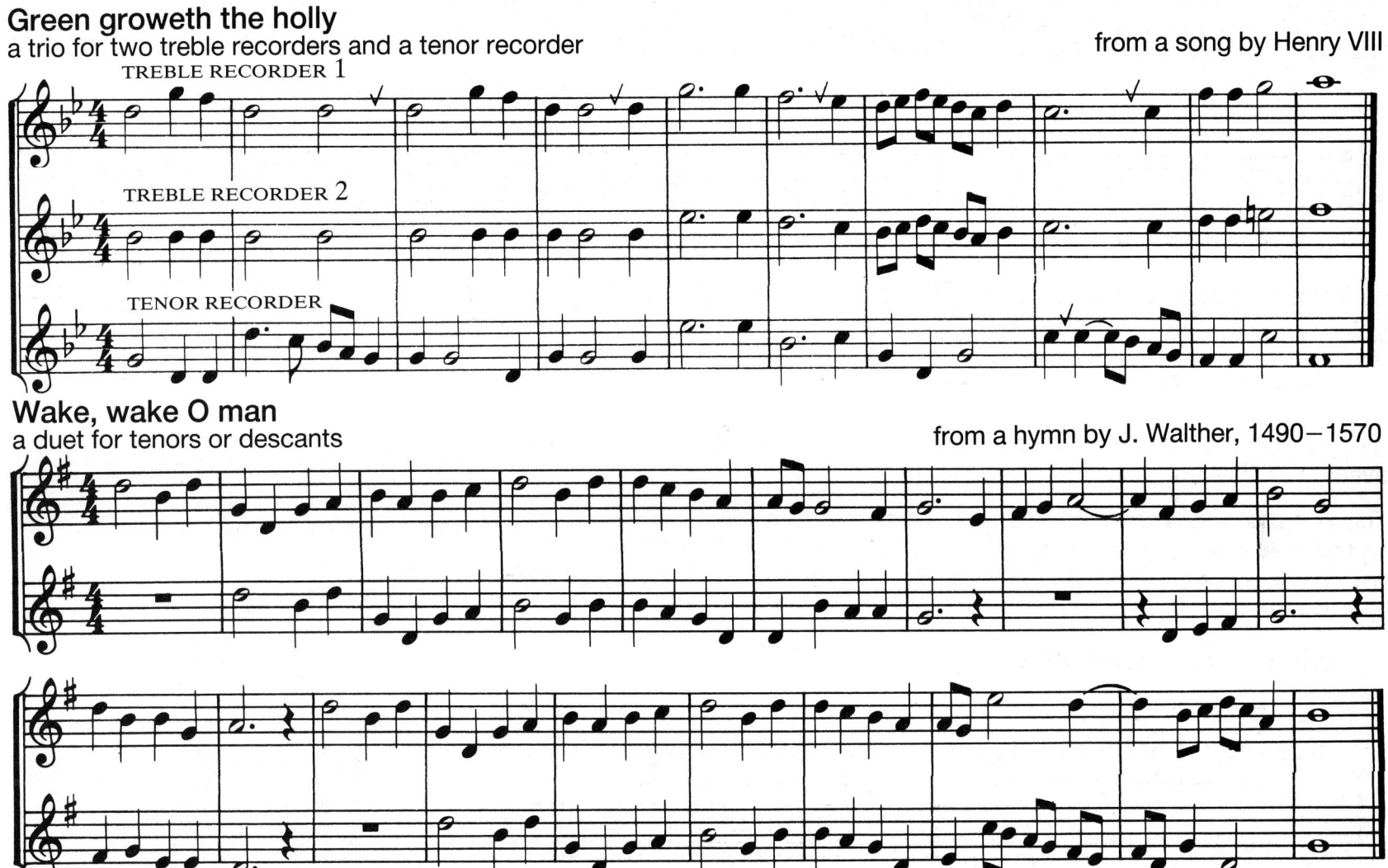

The Spanish pavane

Descant 1
Descant 2 or tenor recorder
Drum

from A. de Cabazon, 1500 ′ 1566

This is a court dance. Perhaps King Henry's Spanish wife, Catherine of Aragon, enjoyed dancing it with the ladies and gentlemen of her household.

Drum beat introduction and throughout:

If you would like to dance the Spanish pavane first try these basic steps for both the pavanes in this book.

1   A simple (S) which means: take one step, then place feet together (close). SL means step left and close, SR means step right and close.
2   A double (D) which means: take three steps and close. DF means a double walking forwards, DB means a double walking backwards.
3   A reverence is a slow deep bow or curtsy, and every dance should start and finish with a reverence to the King or Queen or to the most important person present.

Suggested steps for the Spanish pavane

Find a partner and prepare to dance together clockwise round the hall.
              Reverence.
Bars 1–4:   SL, SR, DF. The music is repeated, and you dance SR, SL, DB.
Bars 5–8:   Take four quick light steps forward, then make a small reverence; repeat this.
Bars 9–10:   SL, SR.
Bars 11–12: A deep reverence.

Musicians

For a reverence, play the first chord of the music (in this case a G chord). Hold the chord for two bars.

Ah, Robin

Voices 1
Treble recorder
Guitar, xylophone (D, E♭, F, G, A) or voices 2

William Cornish, c. 1468 – c. 1523

In 1520 a great meeting of peace and friendship was planned between King Francis I of France and Henry VIII of England. Henry met Francis on the 'Field of the Cloth of Gold', where they had much feasting with wrestling, tournaments, and musical diversions. Henry took with him a large group of musicians, including William Cornish, who wrote this song and who was in charge of ten choirboys, each allowed two pence a day for their food and drink. But England and France were back at war within two years, and again twenty-five years later, when Henry went to Portsmouth to inspect his warships. It was on this occasion that he saw his great ship, the *Mary Rose*, keel over and sink to the bottom of the Solent.

The lower line of this music sounds well on treble recorders, accompanying the voices. A third line is provided too, for guitar plucking single notes, or xylophone, or a second group of voices.

Guitar, xylophone or voice accompaniment

8

An almain for dancing

The almain could be a rather clumpish dance.

Descant recorder 1
Descant recorder 2 or tenor recorder
Guitar or xylophone (D, E, F♮, G, A)
Drum

Attaignant, 16th century dance book

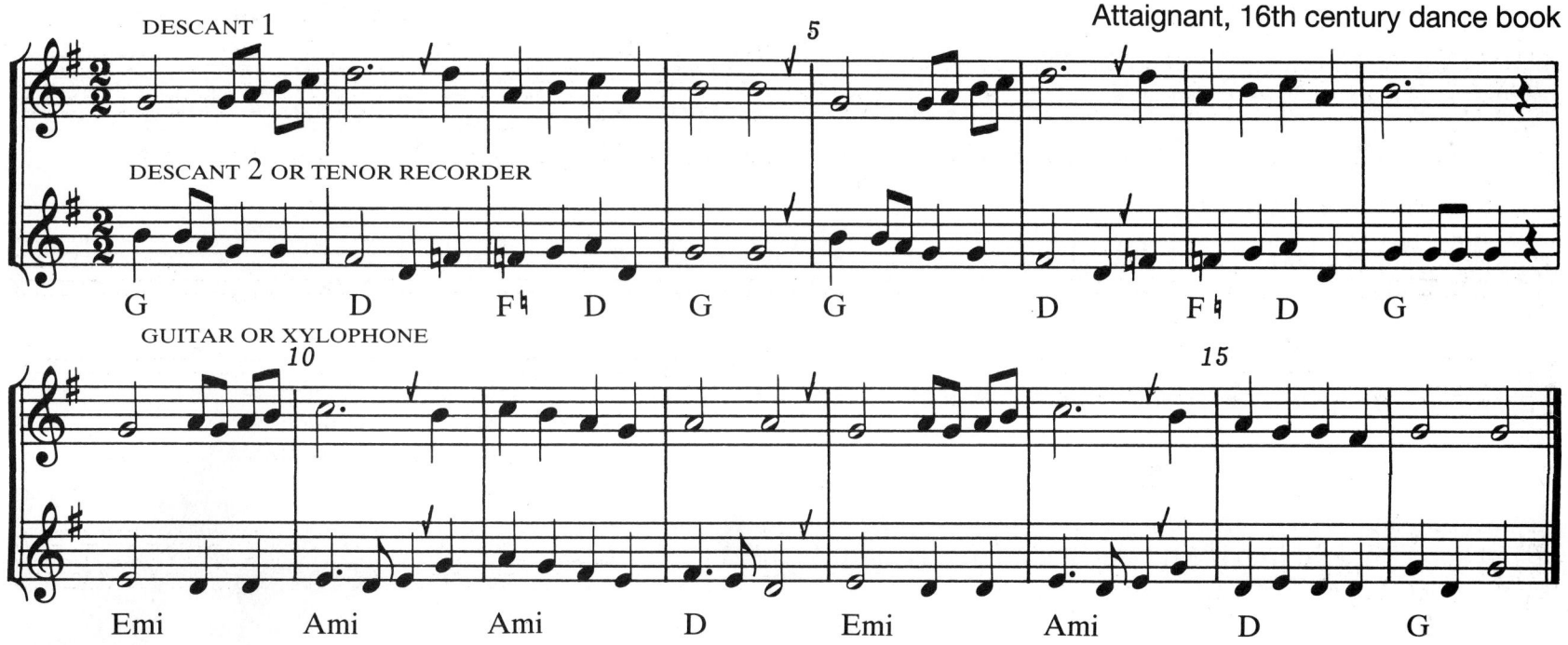

Steps for the almain

Partners stand facing each other in a big circle, men with backs to centre.
Reverence.

Bars 1 – 4: Join both hands with your partner and circle clockwise on the spot: one, two, three, hop, one, two, three, stop. When you hop, bring your leg up in front of you, knee bent and point your toe.

Bars 5 – 8: Now anti-clockwise: one, two, three, hop, one, two, three, stop.

Bars 9 – 16: Men on the inside of the circle holding their lady's hand, dance clockwise round the hall: one, two, three, hop – four times. Reverence.

Play the almain at a comfortable speed for the basic step of the dance:

one, two, three, hop.

Drum rhythm:

9

Mattachins

music for a mock battle

Arbeau's Orchesography, 1589

DESCANT RECORDERS

'Mattachins', a dance with wooden swords, should begin with a parade of sword dancers round the hall. Work out the movements of the actual dance very carefully to avoid confusion and 'blood-shed'.

Make a backing for the tune with as many clattering sounds as you can think of, but keep the rhythm pattern clear and do not drown the tune.

Violinists can turn their bows over and tap open G and D strings with the stick (col legno), in this rhythm:

A part for xylophones

The hunt is up

Voices
Xylophones, glockenspiels or chime bars (D, E, G, A)
Violins

Anon

1 The hunt is up, - the hunt is up, - And it ___ is well - nigh day, _____ And

Har - ry our King is gone a - hunt - ing To bring - his deer ___ to bay! _____

2 The horses snort to be at the sport,
The dogs are running free,
The woods rejoice at the merry noise
Of 'hey tan-ta-ra-tee-ree!'

3 Awake, all men, I say again,
Be merry as you may,
For Harry our King is gone a - hunting
To bring his deer to bay!

Xylophones, glockenspiels or chime bars

Violins

11

𝔄 special entertainment

Your music and dances for Henry VIII might end with a special entertainment called a **masque** or a **disguising**, in which the King himself liked to take part, wearing a mask.

While the musicians play one of their tunes from this book, or a jester dances and tells jokes, the King and a small group of courtiers slip away and put on masks to disguise themselves.

Suddenly there is a loud knocking at the door and a voice cries 'the masked dancers are here!'

To the music of 'An almain for dancing' (page 9), the King and his fellow masked dancers enter and parade round the hall, bowing to the company.

Now come the **revels** when each masked dancer chooses a partner from among the spectators, and they dance 'the almain' together. Then they take off their masks and everyone can see who the maskers were, if they hadn't guessed already.

A 'Mattachins' sword dance (page 10), could follow the revels. It could be a mock jousting tournament too, if the dancers rode on hobbyhorses.

'The hunt is up' (page 11), a song for everyone, could bring the entertainment to an end.

Queen Elizabeth I on progress

Queen Elizabeth, like her father, was a powerful ruler. She was a popular Queen, partly because it was a time of peace and prosperity, but also because she travelled about England and could be seen by everyone. She moved, like Henry, from palace to palace, but also made visits 'on progress' to the great houses of England in the summer months as she liked to get away from London in the hot weather when the plague was about. The nobles and gentry competed with each other in providing splendid entertainments for their Queen.

She usually rode on horseback, even when she was quite old, as the roads were bumpy and carriages had no springs. Packhorses and as many as 300 waggons carried her furniture, bedding, and kitchen utensils when she travelled.

Like her father, Elizabeth enjoyed music and dancing:

She takes great pleasure in dancing and music. She told me she employed at least sixty musicians; in her youth she danced very well and composed measures and music and had played them herself and danced them. She takes such pleasure in it that when her maids dance she follows the cadence with her hand and foot. She rebukes them if they do not dance to her liking and without doubt she is mistress of the art having learnt in the Italian manner to dance high.

from a letter from De Maisse to King Henry IV of France, 1598

Music for a grand procession

the Queen arrives

Descant recorder 1
Descant recorder 2 or tenor recorder
Drum

Bransle, from Gervaise, 1555

[A] DESCANT 1

DESCANT 2 OR TENOR RECORDER

[B]

Walking slowly and with dignity takes some practice. Queen Elizabeth I and her courtiers, ministers, bishops and noblemen would do it to perfection.

The music can quite easily be learned by heart, so the musicians could walk in procession too.

This music should sound very bold, like a fanfare of trumpets. It needs good drumming, perhaps a simple four-in-a-bar introduction to set the speed, then a more complex pattern as the procession moves on its way. Play [A] , [B] twice then [A] again. For variety, two soloists might play [B] the first time, with everyone joining in the repeat. You might add more percussion for the repeat of [A].

Now, Oh now

a courtly song

Voices
Tenor recorders
Tenor recorder 1 or treble or descant recorder
Tenor recorder 2

Music by John Dowland, 1597

Now, O now I needs must part, Part-- ing makes my sad heart mourn.

TENOR RECORDERS

Ab - sence can no joy im - part, Joy once fled can - not re - turn. _____

TENOR 1 OR TREBLE OR DESCANT ONLY

TENOR 2 ONLY

Ab - sence can no joy im - part, Joy once fled can - not re - turn. _____

The Frog galliard

from Thomas Morley's Consorts, 1599

Several foreign princes wanted to marry Queen Elizabeth I and so take control of the kingdom. For six years the French Duc d'Alençon courted her; she called him her 'Froggie'. When he finally returned to France the song 'Now, O now I needs must part' became a dance tune, 'The Frog galliard'.

Tambourine or claves with the recorders will give this a crisp rhythm. Practise changing from 'one two three, four five six' to 'one two, three four, five six'. Give the tambourine a triumphant shake to finish the tune off.

A pavane for dancing

The pavane was a slow, stately dance.

Descant recorder 1   Guitar
Descant recorder 2
Tenor recorder
Drum

Ballo Inglese, Phalèse, 1583

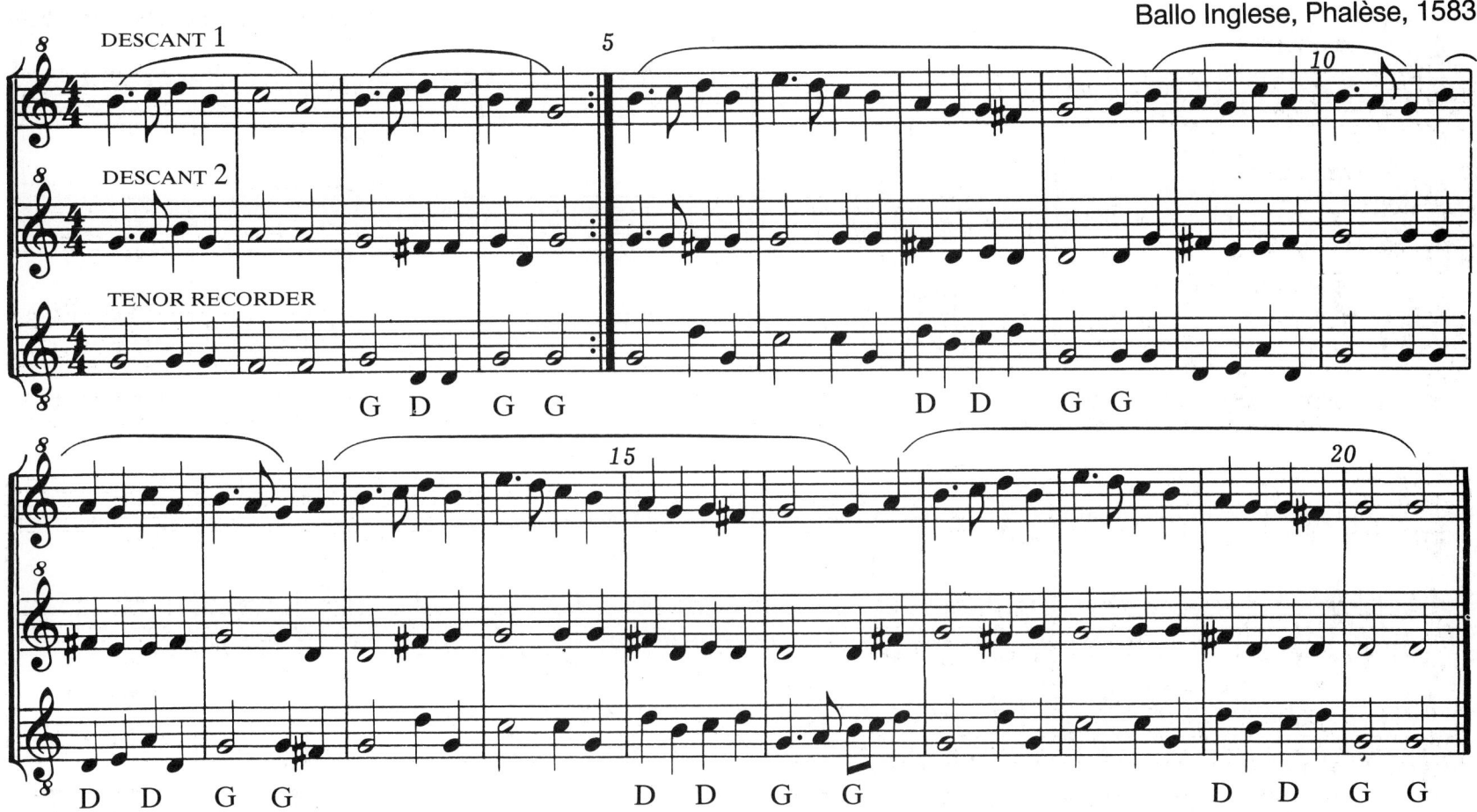

Steps for the pavane   See page 7 for the basic steps

Group in threes, well spaced out in the centre of the hall. Reverence.
SL, SR, DF.
SR, SL, DB.
Repeat these steps until the end of the dance. Reverence.

Play the reverence chord (G) first,
then a drum introduction of two bars.
The mood of a pavane should be smooth and calm.
Guitar chords are provided.

La volta

a favourite dance of Queen Elizabeth I

Melody from Wm. Byrd, Fitzwilliam Virginal Book

G   G   G   D   G   G   D   G   G   G   Ami   G   G   G   D   G

'La volta' was really a dance for one couple, but here is a version which several couples can dance.

Tambourine rhythm as an introduction and throughout:

Steps for 'La volta'

Circle the hall clock-wise, men on the inside, ladies on the outside, holding inside hands.

1   Both spring to the left, then spring to the right. Then take three little runs forward, and pause, twice.

Spring to the left,   spring to the right,   run, run, run, pause, 2, 3, run,   run, run,   pause, 2, 3.

Repeat all this to the repeat of the music.

2   Face your partner, the man's hands round the lady's waist, her hands on his shoulders. Both bend knees, and she jumps high as he lifts her. Join hands and circle on the spot for six counts. Repeat this.

Bend knees and jump!   Round 2,   3, 4,   5, 6.   Bend knees and jump!   Round 2, 3,   4, 5, 6.

Repeat the dance from the start, be careful not to get all bunched in the centre of the hall, so spread well out in a big circle. Of course you begin and end the dance with a reverence to the Queen.

Philip my sparrow

Voices
Treble recorder
Xylophone (D, E, F♮, G, A, Bb)
Bells

John Bartlett, 16th century

Of all the birds that I do know, Phil - ip my spar - row hath no peer,
For sit she high or sit do she low Be she far off or be she near

There is no bird so fair so fine Nor yet so fresh as this of mine, For when she

once hath felt the fit, Phil- ip will cry still yet yet yet yet yet yet yet yet yet yet yet yet yet yet yet!

'Philip' in this case must be short for 'Philippa', rather a long name for a small bird.

The song should go at a hopping, chirrupy speed. Perhaps you could add a little sound of bells now and then to imitate the bells on Philip's perch.

A treble recorder doubling the top line and a xylophone the lower line could support the voices.

Bonny sweet Robin

a duet for treble and tenor recorders

Treble recorder
Tenor recorder
Guitar

Anon

A mi G A mi A mi A mi G A mi E mi A mi D G A mi E mi A mi G A mi

'My Robin is to the greenwood gone . . . For bonny sweet Robin was all my joy.' This folk song was popular in the sixteenth century.

Robert Dudley, Earl of Leicester, was Master of the Queen's Horse and was one of Queen Elizabeth's favourites. She called him 'Robin'.

This song sounds well on treble and tenor recorders, played smoothly and at a gentle speed. As the tune is short try playing just the melody alone first, then repeat it with the lower line as well.

Guitar chords are provided.

More tunes for treble recorders can be found on pages 5 and 8.

The boar's head

a carol for a Tudor Christmas

Voices
Descant or sopranino recorders
Violins
Tenor recorders

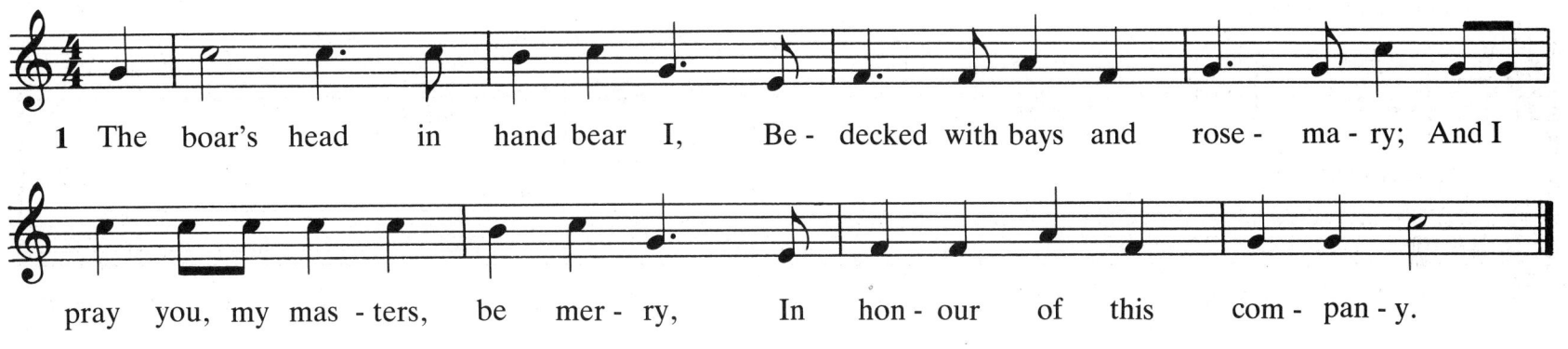

1 The boar's head in hand bear I, Be - decked with bays and rose - ma - ry; And I

pray you, my mas - ters, be mer - ry, In hon - our of this com - pan - y.

CHORUS

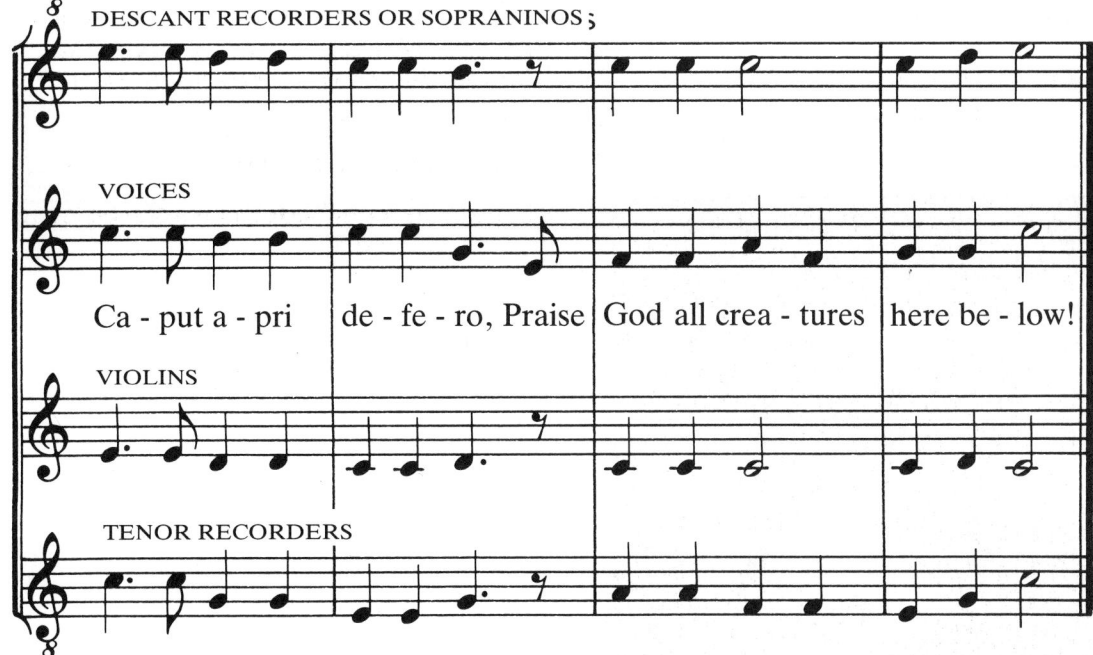

DESCANT RECORDERS OR SOPRANINOS;

VOICES

Ca - put a - pri | de - fe - ro, Praise | God all crea - tures | here be - low!

VIOLINS

TENOR RECORDERS

2 The boar's head, as I understand,
Is the finest dish in all the land.
Our steward hath provided this
In honour of the King of Bliss.

Caput apri, etc.

A tenor recorder playing with the voices will support the tune in the verses. Sing at a dignified, processional speed.

21

Will Kemp's jig

Either: Descant recorder 1
Descant recorder 2 or glockenspiel
Tabor or drum
Bells

Or: Sopranino 1
Sopranino 2 or glockenspiel
Tabor or drum
Bells

Arrangement for two descant recorders, or descant and glockenspiel

from Playford's English Dancing Master

Will Kemp was famous for his morris dancing, so add the sound of the bells he wore strapped to his legs.

He was also an actor in Shakespeare's theatre but he kept adding more and more unscripted jokes to his part, which made Shakespeare so angry that Kemp was sacked from the company.

After he left the theatre Will Kemp made a bet with any Londoners who would take him on that he would dance all the way from London to Norwich. And he did!

A light and lively tabor or drum rhythm is needed for this jig, perhaps ♩ ♪ ♪ ♪ with ♫♫ ♩ ♪ for the last bar in each section.

22

Arrangement for two sopranino recorders, or sopranino and glockenspiel

Chimney sweep's song

from Orlando Gibbons' Cries of London

Voices
Descant recorders
Tenor recorders

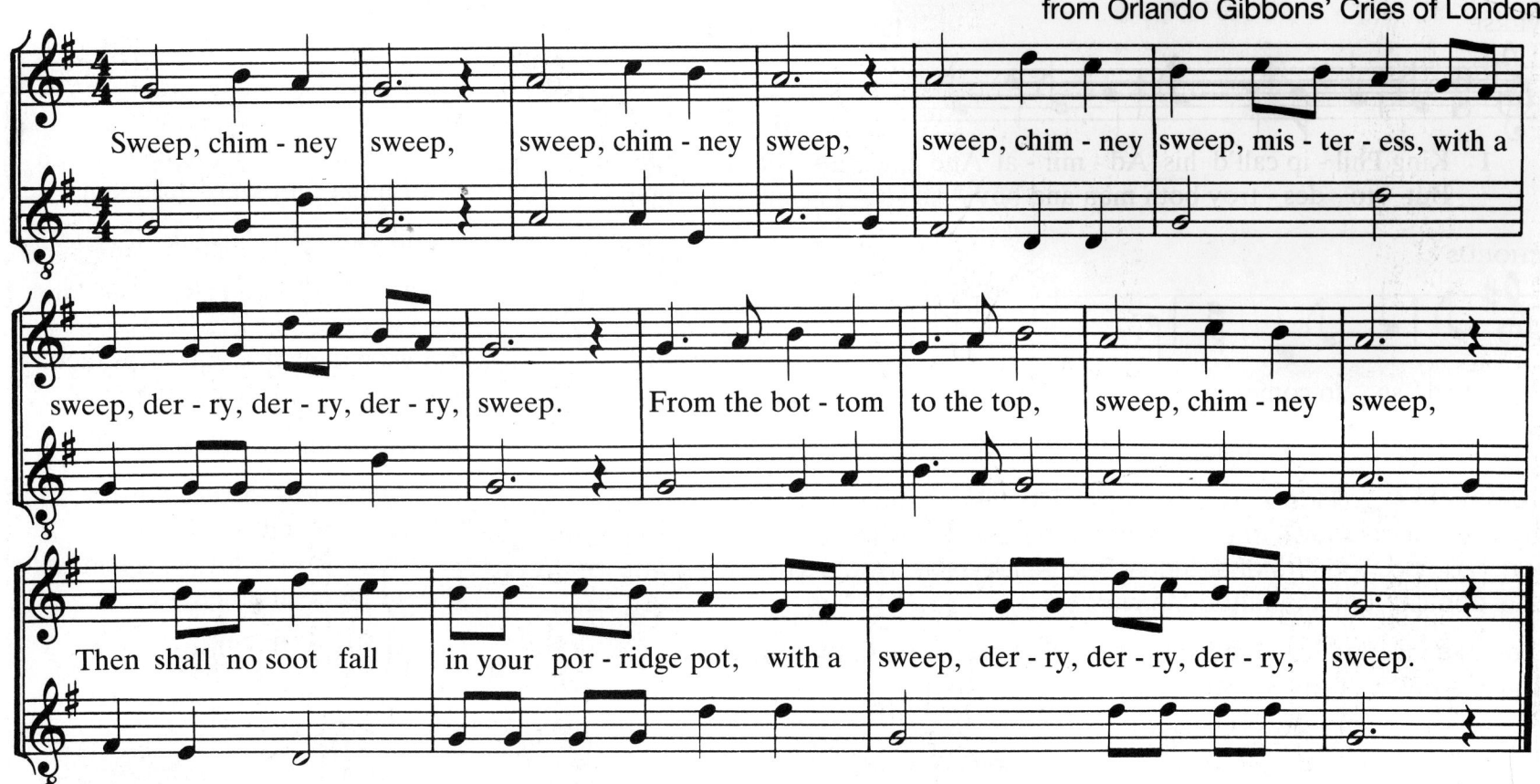

Sweep, chim - ney sweep, sweep, chim - ney sweep, sweep, chim - ney sweep, mis - ter - ess, with a

sweep, der - ry, der - ry, der - ry, sweep. From the bot - tom to the top, sweep, chim - ney sweep,

Then shall no soot fall in your por - ridge pot, with a sweep, der - ry, der - ry, der - ry, sweep.

Here are some more Tudor street cries for a busy market place:

Doublets, ho, any old doublets?

Rats or mice to kill?

Ripe walnuts, ripe!

Live eels, live! Fresh oysters, oysters!

What lack ye? Here are scented gloves!

Any work for the tooth-drawer?

Hot gingerbread, hot!

Knives to grind, any knives to grind?

Hot mutton pies!

The lower line of the music goes well on tenor recorders. You might like to play the tune first on descant and tenor recorders, then the descant players could join the other voices, with tenor accompaniment.

25

Armada ballad

VERSE

tune 'Millfield', from Playford

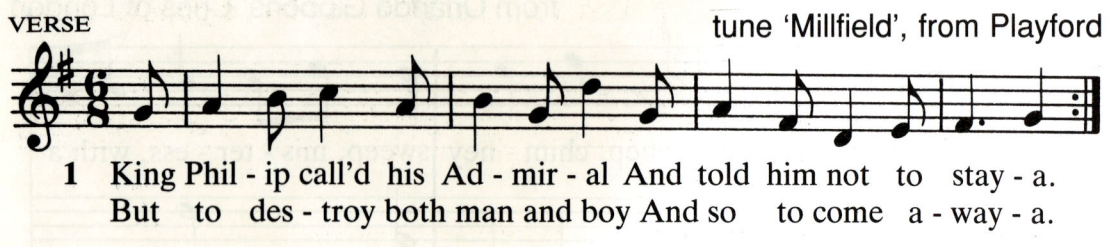

1 King Phil - ip call'd his Ad - mir - al And told him not to stay - a.
But to des - troy both man and boy And so to come a - way - a.

CHORUS

And so to come a - way - a, And so to come a - way - a.

Broad-sheet ballads were poems quickly printed and sold in the streets. They told people the news of the day about battles, trials and executions, or about witches and wonders of all kinds. The ballad-seller would sing the poems to any popular tune that fitted the words.

You can imagine how news about the Spanish Armada being defeated would make a ballad everyone would want to buy.

2 Their navy was well victuall - ed
With biscuit, pease and bacon,
They'd many a gun to make us run
But I think they were mistaken.

I think they were mistaken, etc.

3 They coasted round about our land,
And so came in by Dover,
But we had men set on them then,
And threw the rascals over.

And threw the rascals over, etc.

4 The Queen was then at Tilbury,
What more could we desire - a?
Sir Francis Drake for her sweet sake
Did set them all on fire - a.

Did set them all on fire - a, etc.

Brave Lord Willoughby

a march for the Queen's soldiers

tune from 'Lord Willoughby', a popular ballad

Every village in England had to have men and weapons ready to be used 'within an hour's warning', in case the Spanish Armada landed on the English coast.

Drum introduction, and throughout:

Country people at work

Tinker's song

Tune from R. Deering's Country Cries

I am Tom Tink - er as you may well see, Tink - a - tink - tink with my ham - mer, that's me.

I'll mend your ket - tle, your skil - let or pan, No one can ham - mer as fast as I can!

The tinker could mark the rhythm of his song with his own hammer on an old pan lid.

Country servants' work in winter time

When icicles hang by the wall,
And Dick the shepherd blows his nail,
And Tom brings logs into the hall,
And milk comes frozen home in pail;
When blood is nip't and ways be foul,
Then nightly sings the staring owl
Tu-whit, tu-who! a merry note,
While greasy Joan doth keel the pot.

William Shakespeare

A poem to recite and mime.

A beggars' play

Many beggars tramped along the lanes of Tudor England. Some were genuine cripples, blind people, or wounded soldiers and sailors who could not work, but some were fakes. They were thieves who painted false wounds on their arms and legs and stole whatever they could — clothes from the washing-line, chickens from the farmyard, purses from customers in a crowded market.

They spoke a secret language of their own and were called by such names as:

hookers (thieves who stole clothing out of windows by using hooked sticks)

clappendoggens (fake cripples)

lullaby cheats (infant and child beggars)

bawdy baskets (female pedlars selling stolen goods)

priggers of prancers (horse stealers)

Make up a short play about beggars arriving in the market place. Some will be genuine, some clever fakes. Housewives and shopkeepers will be sorry for them all, until they find out which are thieves in disguise.

A Justice of the Peace was appointed in each parish to give people in real trouble a licence to beg, and to put false beggars in the stocks. Put him into your play too. If a beggar says he was one of Sir Francis Drake's sailors the Justice can ask him questions to find out whether he is lying.

Jog on, jog on

A jig from Playford

Musicians can play this beggars' jig to help the different beggars to act their parts. Play it very slowly for crippled beggars, or for the thieves as they prowl around stealthily stealing, but quite fast while the thieves brag and skip around showing each other their loot.

Use different percussion for different beggars, for example, drums for the real beggars, wood blocks and scrapers for the fakes.

29

The clog brawl

a circle dance for town or country folk

Descant recorder 1
Descant recorder 2 or tenor recorder
Xylophone (C, F, G, top C)
Mixed percussion

Arbeau, 1589

This is a miming dance for bakers, farm workers, tailors, housewives, dairywomen, falconers and anyone who wants to join in.

Steps for the clog brawl

Make a circle and join hands.

Bars 1–4: All take three steps clockwise and turn, three steps anti-clockwise and turn. Repeat this to the repeat of the music.

Bar 5: Everyone plants their left heel into the middle of the circle.

Bar 6: Then their right heel.

Bar 7: Then all stamp three times.

Now the miming starts. The first part of the dance (bars 1 – 4) is always the same, but instead of the first heel-tapping the bakers could show us how they kneed the dough for bread, then instead of the second heel-tapping everybody copies the bakers, then everyone stamps three times.

Each time the dance is repeated a different group of people mime their trade.

The music should be played briskly: ♩ = 88.

During bars 5 and 6 you could use contrasting percussion instruments, for example, claves the first bar, drum the second.

Notes and suggestions for teachers

Henry VIII at Hampton Court

The music in this section has been chosen to illustrate King Henry's interest in hunting, singing, dancing and jousting, and to provide examples of the amusements of his court.

Ways to use this music
To put your topic work together as a dramatic presentation you might first recreate the scene of bustle and last-minute preparation before the King arrives at Hampton Court. A steward would direct the servants, among them grooms and falconers, to provide for the King's hunting in the park. The Master of the King's Music would make sure the musicians were quite ready and had some of the King's own music to play and sing.

page 3   *Music for the King's entry* sounds splendidly regal if played at a dignified speed. Make a feature of impressive drumming first, for at least four bars.

page 4   *Pastime with good company*   Avoid descant recorders playing with the voices if you can; use descants for an instrumental version, then support the voices with a tenor recorder, it blends better.

page 5   *Green groweth the holly*   If this trio is played with just one recorder to a part the players can really listen to each other and play in tune.
Wake, wake O man   We have supplied a decorated ending with quaver runs, in the manner of Tudor musicians showing off their skill.

page 6   *The Spanish pavane* makes a good formal first dance. The staccato markings are only a suggestion, phrase the music as you think best. The whole class might practise some simples and doubles to this music, to give them the feeling of the formality and dignity of a courtly dance.

page 8   *Ah, Robin* in the original is a complex sort of round. Here we have picked out three lines of William Cornish's music and put them together more simply. Start with the voices, perhaps with a tenor recorder, then sing the song again twice with the treble recorder line added, then twice more with the guitar/xylophone line as well.

page 9   *An almain for dancing*   Hand-held masks look good but dancers cannot then join hands for the almain.

page 10   *Mattachins*   A sword dance or mock jousting tournament will have to be carefully worked out, and should be very formal; gestures rather than swipes with the sword. Hobbyhorses could be either the pole-and-head variety or, more authentically, the kind that sits on the hips.

page 11   *The hunt is up* makes a good final song for everyone to join in, and the King might then announce that he expects to see all his courtiers in the saddle ready to hunt with him next day at dawn!

You might like to add a Tudor poem to your Hampton Court entertainment. This one is by John Skelton, 1460 – 1529.

Merry Marg'ret,
As midsummer flower,
Gentle as falcon,
Or hawk of the tower,

With solace and gladness,
Much mirth and no madness

Is Merry Marg'ret
As midsummer flower,
*Gentle as falcon,
Or hawk of the tower.

                     *Gentle = well-bred, as in gentleman

page 12   *A special entertainment*   Masques or disguisings of this kind were very popular, probably because they allowed a little more licence in the choice of dancing partner than was normally permitted. Masks are always fun to make and look spectacular, especially if they are sprayed with gold or silver paint, and are well decorated round the edge, for example, with strips of curled paper. Try making animal masks, signs of the zodiac, half-white and half-black masks, grotesques, feathered faces: all should be large and easily wearable for dancing.

Queen Elizabeth I on progress

Ways to use this music
As the Queen frequently went on progress to visit the great houses of her richest subjects, you might like to present your music and dances in the form of an entertainment for the Queen on progress during her visit to such a household.

Again, there would be much busy preparation, with a steward in charge, but here preparations can 'act out' what the children have been learning about Tudor housekeeping; roasting meat on a spit, brewing ale, the use of herbs for cooking, medicine or 'sweetening' rooms, bee-keeping, butter-making, etc.

At this point you might like to use 'The chimney sweep song' from the next section (page 25), or the poem 'Country servants' work in winter time' (page 28).

The owners of the great house the Queen is to visit, perhaps a Lord and his Lady, would stand ready by the door to greet her, along with such upper servants as the steward and the chaplain and tutor to the Lord's children.

page 14   *Music for a grand procession*   The Queen enters the hall to this music and walks in procession to the dais and a special chair made ready for her.

If you are lucky and have some trumpet or cornet players in your school their teacher will probably be willing to provide a simple fanfare for them to play to announce the Queen's arrival, before she enters the hall. To arrive to the sound of trumpets was the special privilege of royalty.

page 15   *Now, O now*   This sad song of parting was the result of a quarrel between the Queen and the Earl of Essex. He wrote the words, the melody is by John Dowland.

The song is easy to learn provided the children have plenty of practice in grouping six beats in a bar as either '**one** two three, **four** five six' or '**one** two, **three** four, **five** six'. Practise clapping or with percussion instruments. Then the penultimate bar in each section will give no trouble.

page 16   *The Frog galliard*   As you can see the melody is that of the song 'Now, O now', and the rhythm pattern is the same too.

page 17   *A pavane for dancing*   The lines over the music are to help the players with the phrasing and to encourage them to play smoothly. The pavane sounds well on recorders, especially with some guitar chords as marked, but if you have good string players available, use a band of violins, or violins, violas and 'cellos.

To add drama to the dance you might have four torch-bearers entering first, and standing at each corner of the hall. If dancing in threes, the middle dancer of each three might wear a golden mask or an ornamental head-dress.

page 18   *La volta*   is always a favourite, especially if a teacher dances with the children and lifts his partner really high in the air. Before learning the dance read aloud the extract about the Queen dancing (page 13).

page 19   *Philip my sparrow*   is a good song for the younger members of the household. Vary the dynamics of 'yet, yet, yet, yet', either starting softly and getting louder or beginning boldly and fading away to nothing.

page 20   *Bonny sweet Robin*   Sadly only a few of the old words for this song remain, but it is a beautiful tune and suits the softer tone of treble and tenor recorders. It is well worth finding a guitarist to play with them.

page 21   *The boar's head*   carol is useful for a Christmas event. It appears in a 15th century manuscript, and is still sung every year at the Queen's College, Oxford.